RESTART VIOLIN

Written by Helena Ruinard

WISE PUBLICATIONS
part of The Music Sales Group

London / New York / Paris / Sydney / Copenhagen / Berlin / Madrid / Hong Kong / Tokyo

Published by
Wise Publications
14-15 Berners Street, London W1T 3LJ, UK.

Exclusive Distributors:
Music Sales Limited
Distribution Centre, Newmarket Road,
Bury St Edmunds, Suffolk IP33 3YB, UK.
Music Sales Pty Limited
20 Resolution Drive, Caringbah, NSW 2229, Australia.

Order No. AM1002837
ISBN: 978-1-84938-974-7
This book © Copyright 2012 Wise Publications,
a division of Music Sales Limited.

Author: Helena Ruinard.
Project editor: Lizzie Moore.
Book design: Camden Music.
Photography: Matthew Ward.
Violin played by Helena Ruinard.
CD mixed and mastered by Jonas Persson.
Cover design by Tim Field.
Cover photograph courtesy of Robert Kneschke/Timothy Large - Fotolia.

Printed in the EU.

**For access to the complementary piano accompaniments for this book, go to
www.hybridpublications.com and enter the code VE398.**

Introduction

Congratulations on making the decision to return to the violin! This book is designed to stimulate and satisfy an appetite for music-making. There are tips on how to practise every piece in order to help you get pleasing results. You will get more out of the book with a teacher but the aim is to enable you to enjoy playing, not to turn you into a virtuoso.

This book assumes an intermediate level of playing and musical knowledge—around Grade 4 standard—but the collection of pieces range from comparatively easy through to intermediate in approximate order of difficulty. It will require some work and patience to get the best results (remember all those hours of practice in your youth?). If something is not working, it is enormously helpful to be able to stand back and work out which factor of your playing needs working on—is it the left hand or the right hand? There are exercises throughout for all the main technical challenges you will meet.

Before you turn over to begin this book, here are some directions and advice on how to go about using it.

Before each piece you will see that there is a section on preparing your performance. The book is designed to get you playing as quickly and successfully as possible. Make sure you read each section before you tackle the music.

These sections include:

- **Scale shapes to practise** These finger patterns show you the diatonic notes which are needed within the designated key.

- **Warm-ups** These handy warm-ups are used to prepare for the expression, technique and articulation needed in the piece. They concentrate on things like bowing, vibrato, scales, fingering and rhythm.

- **Practice windows** These are designed to isolate a few bars at a time in order to get to grips with difficult passages before you come to play the piece through for the first time.

You will also find a theory reminder section at the back of the book (pages 60–63) to be used as a reference and to help with anything you may have forgotten!

Happy music-making!

Daily Workouts

OK, you may not get around to these every day, but they are only really effective if done regularly.

Try doing them at the beginning of each playing session—you will notice a difference in just a few days.

1 **Posture** Being relaxed and balanced is key to a good technique. Start off standing without your instrument. Check you are standing straight with knees unlocked; let your arms hang by your side and relax your shoulders; let the neck muscles loosen so that your head moves freely.

Place the violin on your shoulder and keep the neck and shoulder relaxed by taking some of the weight of the violin with your left hand.

Take up the bow and try to keep the right shoulder relaxed.

2 **Tone** Choose a resonant note—D on the A string is best—and using fairly fast, long bows try to find the optimum speed and weight of bow to make the violin resonate freely and at its fullest volume without forcing the sound. This is called 'tonus'.

Bowing If you maintain good contact with the bow and it stays parallel with the bridge you will get a good sound. Half bows are easier than whole bows so start off in the upper half, then the middle and then the lower half.

Bow Hold

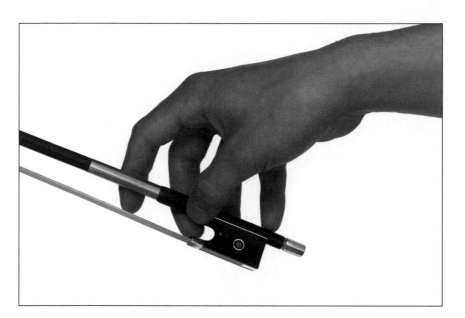

3 **Intonation** First of all, form the hand so that it is playing fourths (also known as the Geminiani chord, see diagram).

 **The Geminiani Chord**

Good tone and good intonation go hand in hand. Play a scale stopping on each note to get it to 'ring'. G major is a good one to start with.

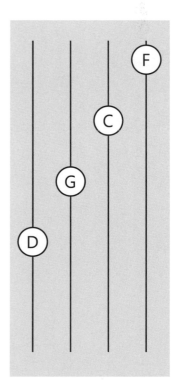

The Geminiani Chord

7

Care Of The Instrument & Advice On Accessories

- Get yourself a good shoulder rest which keeps the violin in place securely and lets your neck and shoulders stay relaxed.

- Buy some good-quality strings and if necessary ask someone experienced to string the violin. When using the pegs to tune, loosen them slightly first and then push them in steadily as you tighten them. If they get stuck or are very stiff, use peg paste. If they don't stay in place, use chalk. There are a number of good makes of string to choose from including Dominant, Pirastro, D'Addario and Corelli.

- Remember to use a soft cloth, or duster, to remove rosin from the strings and violin. This will improve the sound of the strings and keep the varnish in good condition. It is also very important to loosen the bow hair after playing so that the bow does not become warped.

The Can Can

The mood of this first piece is jolly; you can translate this onto the violin by making the quavers *staccato* and using vigorous bow strokes on the longer notes.

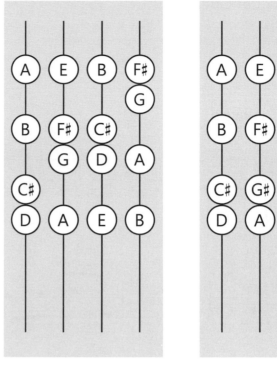

D major   **A major**

Warm-up

Staccato quavers *Staccato* is easiest in the lower half of the bow. Find the balancing point (where the weight of the bow either side is equal) and play short bows on any note, letting the bow bounce naturally. If you find it difficult to make the notes even or to play at tempo this way, simply play short detached notes on the string. Just give them plenty of energy!

Practice windows

Bars 25–26 and 63–64: D major scale and A major scale As this pattern appears four times it is worth making it sound good! Practise it slowly and pay particular attention to the highest note.

Bars 37–38: A simple arpeggio This comes again six bars later.

The Can Can

Music by Jacques Offenbach

Allegro

Largo

As this piece has a nostalgic feel to it, let the bowing be gentle whilst maintaining enough pressure to produce a sweet sound with a little *vibrato*.

It will sound best in third position, providing your fourth finger is strong and independent enough.

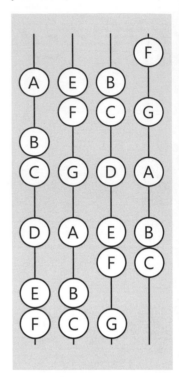

C major

Warm-up 1

Fourth finger strengthening With your left-hand fourth finger, pluck each open string. Go one step further and do the same except keep your first finger down at the same time!

Warm-up 2

Fourth finger vibrato On the A string or the D string, play notes on 0–1–2–3–4, aiming for the same vibrato on each finger.

Practice window

Bar 15: Preparing the fourth finger Retain a physical memory of where the fourth finger went to play the G on beat 2 and during beat 3 make sure it is ready to play the C in the same place on the D string on beat 4.

Largo

Music by Antonín Dvořák

Yesterday

There is an air of resignation to this song and its unhurried lyricism is what makes it so irresistible. Aim for a warm tone without too much vibrato. Use fourth fingers where possible and inject more energy into the chorus (bars 17–24, below) for contrast.

Scale shapes to practise

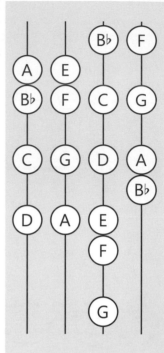

D minor melodic descending

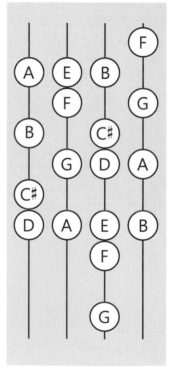

D minor melodic ascending

Practice windows

Bars 7 and 9: Syncopated bowing Syncopation is typical of jazz as well as all sorts of world and pop music, like this song. When string players play jazz they tend to use short, contained bow strokes to make these rhythms more punchy. Try using more pressure and less length in these bars and others like them.

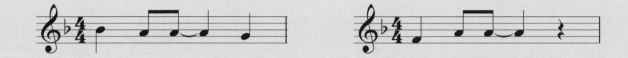

Bars 17–21: Third position This is an opportunity to reacquaint yourself with third position if you need to, although this section (bars 17–24, opposite) can also be played in first position. Bar 19 will need extra care as you prepare your fourth finger to play the C. Refer to the scale shapes opposite to help with placing your fingers.

Yesterday

Words & Music by John Lennon & Paul McCartney

Gently

mp

slower

dim.

Entr'acte

The key to this piece is simplicity. Go easy on the vibrato but aim for a sweet sound.

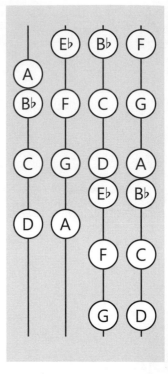

Bb major

Warm-up

Bars 1–2: Up-bows The articulation of the quavers is not just written like that for the sake of being awkward—it is an effective way of emphasising the 'two-time' feel of the piece. Practise playing two up-bows in one, stopping the sound in between.

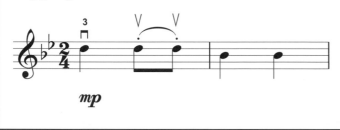

Practice windows

Bars 13–14: Shifts and fingering It is nice to keep the tone even and warm by staying on the A string here. In bar 14 try *shifting up* to second position for the F and *extending* or 'crawling' back down to first position for the D. Use the first finger as your guide, shifting up a tone from Bb to C before playing the F with your fourth finger. This is repeated in bars 45–46.

Bars 33–40: Fourth position

Another practice window

Bars 62–64: Shifts and fingering Bar 62 is a repeat an octave higher of bar 14 and in this case you don't really have any choice but to stay on one string and shift. Similar to bar 14, *shift up* from third position and then *extend* or *'crawl'* back down to third position. Use the second finger as your guide, shifting a major third from B♭ to D before playing the top F with your fourth finger.

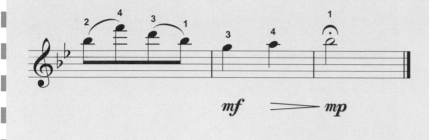

Entr'acte

Music by Franz Schubert

Andantino ♩ = 72

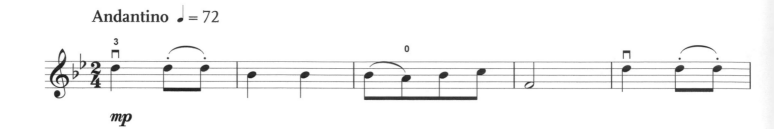

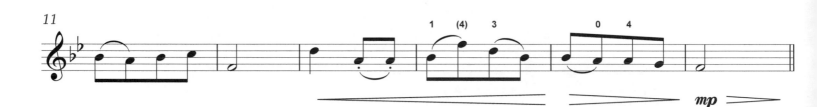

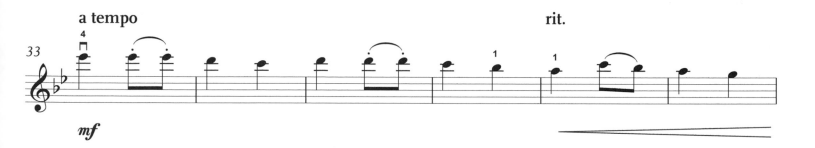

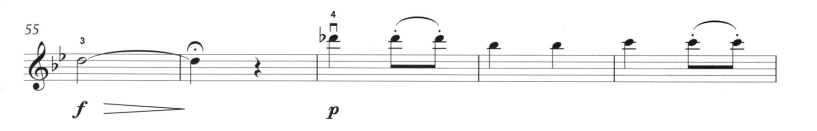

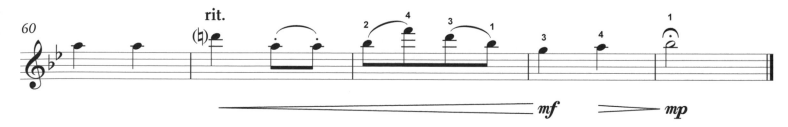

Cabaret

Need some razzle-dazzle? This piece is bound to do the trick. Think of how bright and clear the singers and bands are in musicals—that's what you are going to emulate!

This song has some mild syncopation to keep it sounding jazzy, staccato for extra energy and a lot of *rubato* (when the performer literally 'robs' time from one part of a phrase only to give it back in another, in other words, slows down and speeds up) for expressive effect.

Before attempting to play it with the CD, listen to the demonstration track to hear exactly how the violin part fits in and where and how slow the *ritenuto* and *rubato* passages are. When you come to play it with the CD it would certainly be easier to play it with the demonstration track first instead of the backing track.

Scale shapes to practise

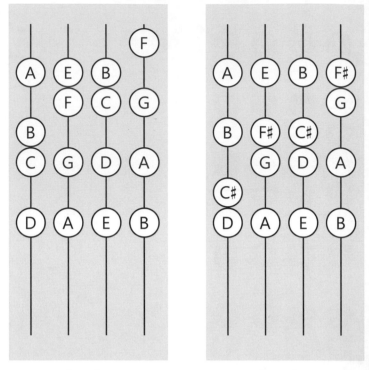

C major　　　　　**D major**

Warm-up

Staccato See similar warm-up for *The Can Can*. Try and keep your fingers loose on the bow so that they are able to act as a kind of 'suspension' for your hand.

Practice window

Bars 7–8: Syncopation, staccato, chromatic note This is the first part of the main theme of the A section, which returns, modified, towards the end of the number, so these are two important bars. Practise getting the syncopation rhythm right with a fast up-bow on the E in bar 8. Don't worry about getting the staccato off the string in these bars—short and detached will do nicely.

More practice windows

Bars 35–39: Staccato and bow control Aim to let the bow bounce for these quavers. For the long held slurred notes, start at the heel and, if necessary, take a little time out of the end of the note to get back to the lower half for the quaver up-beat to the following bar.

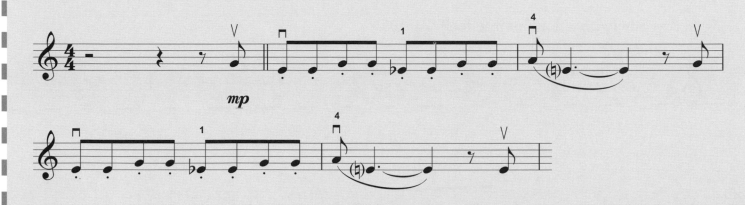

Bars 41–43: Semiquavers in the upper half Playing semiquavers (beginning of bar 42) on an up-bow in the upper half might feel odd but it will get you where you need to be in the bow for the staccato quavers which follow.

23

Cabaret

Words by Fred Ebb & Music by John Kander

25

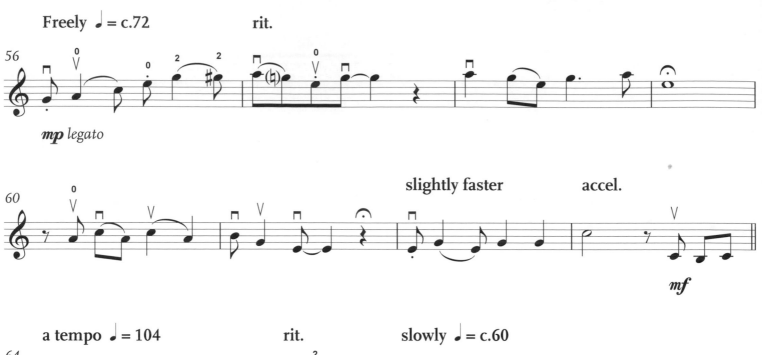

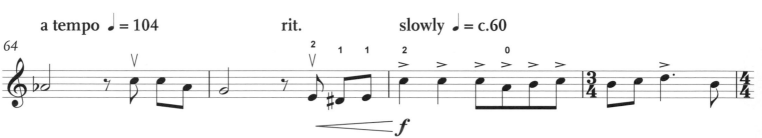

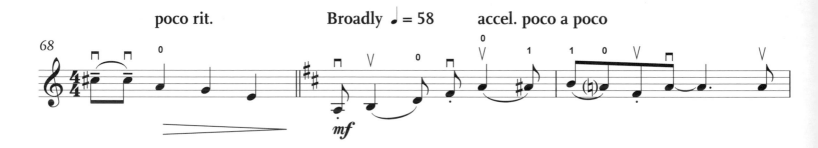

Por Una Cabeza

One of the most popular tangos, this has formed part of the soundtrack to various TV programmes and been featured in films including *Scent Of A Woman*, *Schindler's List*, and *True Lies*. Watching a few YouTube clips should get you in a suitably sultry mood!

The piece is formed of two contrasting sections: the A section (bars 4–20) and the B section (bars 21–36), which appear twice. The rhythm in bars 36–52 is simply a variation of the basic rhythm as it appears in the first A section.

The most important thing is to make sure that the notes which come on beats 1 and 3 sound in time.

Scale shapes to practise

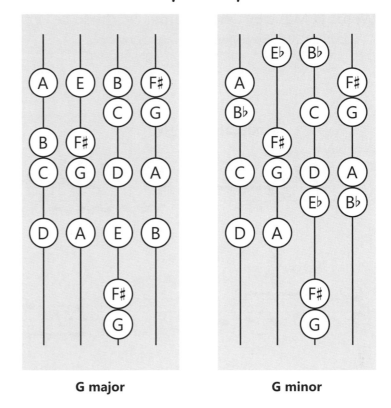

G major   **G minor**

Try taking a little time out of the end of the crotchet to prepare for the semiquavers.

Practice windows

Bars 21–22: Rhythm The three triplet crotchets are to be played in the time of two crotchets. It may look harder than it is—try singing along with a recording and you will have it.

Bars 40–41: Arpeggios Watch out for the C♮ (low third finger) followed by the G♯ (high third finger) in bar 41.

Por Una Cabeza

Words & Music by Carlos Gardel & Alfredo Le Pera

Moderate Tango

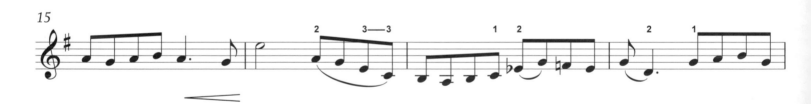

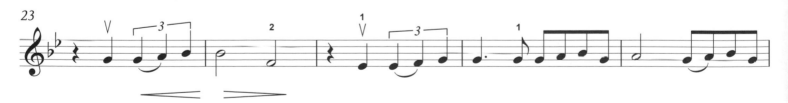

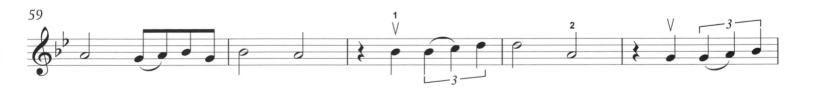

Clair De Lune

Imagine a still, clear moonlit evening—depicted here, in music, like a beautiful impressionist painting. The piece is written in a gently lilting $\frac{9}{8}$ and much of it is to be played softly.

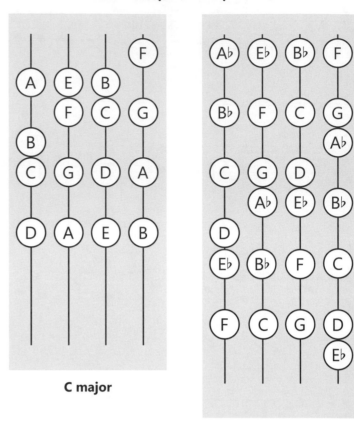

Scale shapes to practise

C major

C minor

Warm-up 1

Metre A failsafe way to count the beats in $\frac{9}{8}$ is:

one - and - a, two - and - a, three - and - a

This way you are keeping track of each quaver as well as a strong sense of the main beats.

Warm-up 2

Bowing Much of this piece needs a soft, breathy tone. Try bowing at different speeds and with different arm weight near the fingerboard. When the music builds up to a healthy *mf* you will need to be using more weight and bowing nearer the bridge, so experiment with different bow speeds and arm weight near the bridge as well.

Practice window

Bars 2–5: Rhythm You may have to play these bars a few times in order to get the feeling of the tie-over beats which means you have to make an extra effort to feel the beats clearly in your head/toes/wherever! The *2* beneath the quavers in bar 4 stands for 'two quavers in the time of three', which is easy if you just concentrate on the three main dotted crotchet beats.

More practice windows

Bars 16–19: Rhythm Similar to the way you approached bars 2–5, practise feeling the beats clearly somewhere in your body. To get used to the **rit.** it may be useful simply to imagine playing it as you are listening to the backing track.

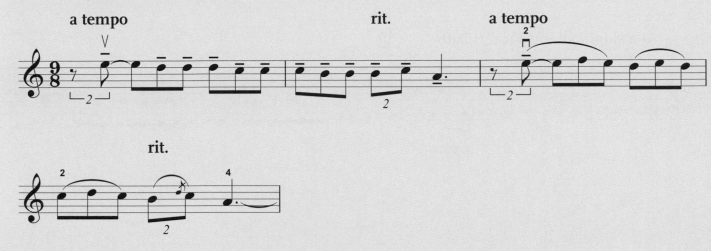

Bars 20–27: Bow control Every other bar is articulated in one long up-bow. You will need to apply slightly more pressure on the bow in order to maintain a similar dynamic to the alternate bars, which are articulated with separate bows. Make every bar a little louder and more urgent than the last.

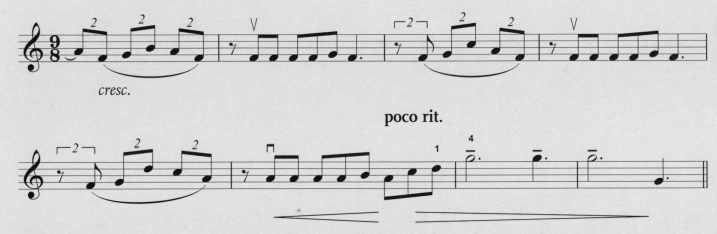

Bars 41–43: Shifts This is only an E♭ major scale, but it may be worth practising so you feel really secure with the shifts.

Clair De Lune

Music by Claude Debussy

At a slow walking pace, rubato ♩. = 50

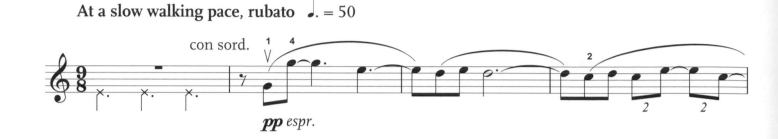

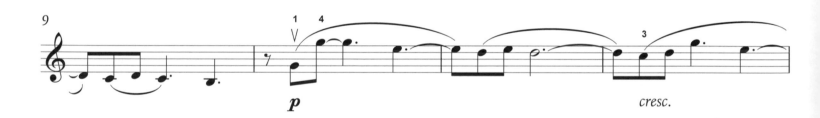

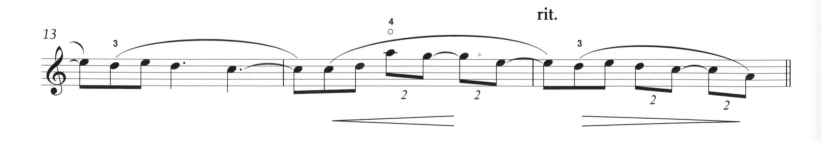

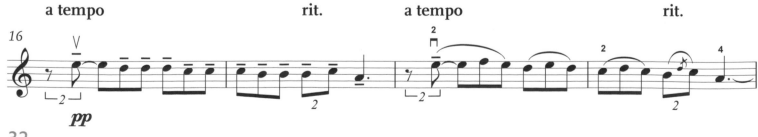

poco rit.

dim.

p

Reflectively, with less pace

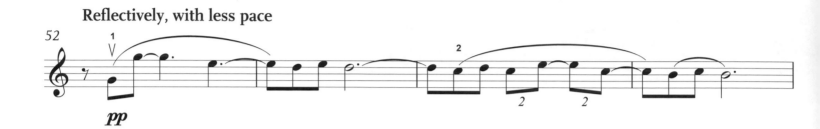

pp

moving on   rit.

moving on   rit. al fine

A Love Before Time

Scale shape to practise

Think 'relaxed Latino ballad' crossed with an expansive film score theme, finished off with the occasional oriental moment. Use lots of bow, be expressive and get into the groove!

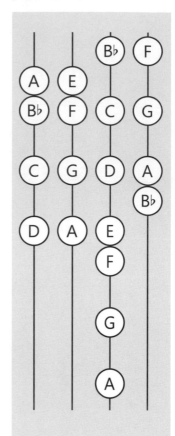

D minor mode

Warm-up

D minor scale A nice simple warm-up—make it two octaves so you can practise your shifts. Play the *melodic minor* if you can remember it or, even better, the *natural minor*.

Practice window

Bars 16 (beat 4)–20 (beat 3): Syncopation and bow control If you make sure your bow speed is evenly paced, you will always have enough left to make long notes expressive right to the end. The more pressing concern for these bars and the piece in general is the syncopation. Just keep counting the main beats and, if necessary, mark them into your music.

Watch out for the D which comes just after the fourth beat of bar 18. Try practising bar 20 using separate bows and *without* ties.

Another practice window

Bars 22 (beat 4)–25: Syncopation and bowing at the point *Punta d'arco* indicates that the music is to be played at the point of the bow, and so is perfect for making a light and airy sound. To play the rhythms at the beginning of bar 23, try bouncing off beats 1 and 2.

Notice how it is effectively the same rhythm as in bar 26. Conversely, to play the rhythm at the end of bar 24 into bar 25, just anticipate beat 3 in bar 24, and beat 2 in bar 25.

A Love Before Time

Words & Music by James Schamus, Tan Dun & Jorge Calandrelli

Latino ballad ♩ = 69

molto cresc.

mf

molto cresc. **f**

punta d'arco

lightly

norm.

mf

punta d'arco

norm.

mp

I Got Rhythm

Scale shape to practise

The clue to this piece is in the title! Think more 'rhythmic' than 'melodic' and keep your bowing contained and punchy. For the introduction, use fast, light bows to bring off the staccato crotchets.

Swung quavers

This means that out of every pair you lengthen the first note and shorten the second so that they are rhythmically closer to triplets than straight quavers.

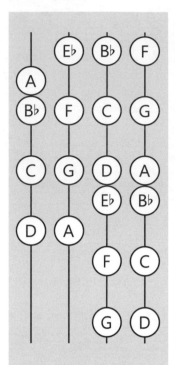

Bb major

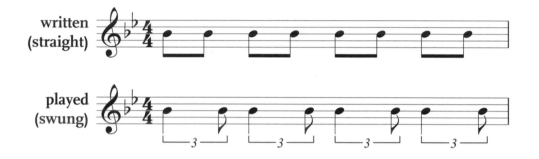

Warm-up

Fifth position It would be worth dusting down the top of your fingerboard and reacquainting yourself with fifth position. Try shifting from third to fifth position using first, second (shift here) and first finger. Raise your hand as you reach fifth position for better facility.

Practice window

Bars 35–36: Rhythm This rhythm is the basis of the whole number, syncopated and with swung quavers. Notice how it goes by quickly on the page because of the minim beats. It is essentially this:

If you find the real version tricky, practise it a few times without the syncopation, as above.

More practice windows

Bars 40–42: Swung quavers There is barely any time to show the swung quavers in the first part of the theme but as soon as the melody develops, as here, bring them out. Practise them straight first, if need be.

Bar 91: Rhythm and fingering Just play this bar slowly and with straight quavers, gradually increasing the tempo and then introducing the swung quavers.

Bars 99–100: Swung quavers

Bars 119–125: Fifth position

I Got Rhythm

Music by George Gershwin

43

Someone To Watch Over Me

Here is another of Gershwin's many hits. It quickly became a jazz standard, covered by many musicians, from Ella Fitzgerald, Oscar Peterson and Stéphane Grappelli to Keith Jarrett and even Lady Gaga. Each of its themes is essentially made up of simple rhythms, but here they are written out in the way that they would be performed: as freely as possible and ideally different each time.

Here is the main theme, which comes round three times and is written differently each time.

Scale shape to practise

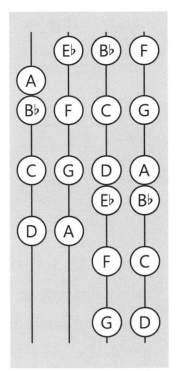

B♭ major

Warm-up 1

Triplet rhythms Playing regular quavers or crotchets and then triplets is like switching between simple time and compound time. Keeping track of the four main beats is paramount!

Try clapping or playing the following rhythm:

Warm-up 2

Crotchet triplets When the time signature is 𝄴 and you are confronted with crotchet triplets, don't panic—there are two ways to approach it. The easy way is to think of the second note as coming just before the second beat, and the third note as coming just after.

The accurate way is to divide the notes into tied quaver-triplets like this:

Practice windows

Bars 5–6: Rhythm The rhythm of these bars is simply a variation on bars 1–2. It may take a little practice to alternate between normal quavers and triplets.

Bars 47–51: Semitone shifts and flourishes Start with the semiquavers at the end of bar 47 and bar 49. Practise them slowly, as each shift is a different distance. The flourishes at the beginning of bar 47 and bar 50 are just that. Technically the triplet semiquavers take the time of a quaver; practically, just play them fast and sing through the long note that comes afterwards.

Someone To Watch Over Me

Music by George Gershwin

mp espressivo

rit.

cresc.

p

A tempo

mp

mf cantabile

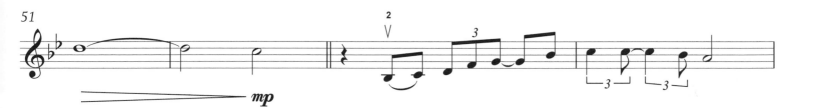

molto rall.

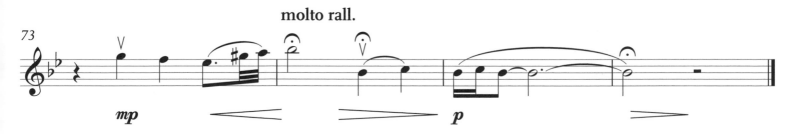

March Of The Toys

The *Nutcracker* is all about the magical joy of a childhood Christmas. As well as communicating that world of delight, this piece is a taut march, which needs to be delivered with as much poise and control as possible!

The dotted-rhythm passages, e.g. bars 29–32, are one of the defining themes of this piece. Whilst they are there to move the music on and have a strong sense of direction, the space between each pair of notes is almost as important as the notes themselves. See if you can take weight off the bow at the same time as leaving the bow on the string during the rests.

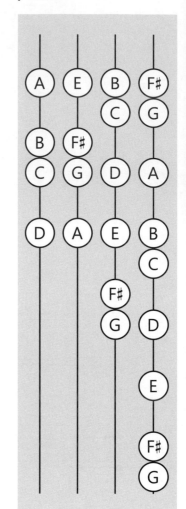

G major

Warm-up 1

G major scale, three octaves This is really to prepare for the last four bars. If you are not comfortable with these dizzy heights just play the last four bars down the octave.

Warm-up 2

Flexible fingers You need flexible right-hand fingers to play staccato. Practise bending and straightening your fingers whilst holding the bow. See if you can produce tiny bow strokes using only your fingers with no arm action.

Practice window

Bars 1–2: Staccato

More practice windows

Bars 18–20: Grace notes As ever, practise each pair of notes slowly first of all. When playing them up to tempo, keep them light and let the second (main) note sound.

Bars 29–32: Bowing at the point Try playing bars 29 and 30 near the point, moving to the middle of the bow during the crescendo. The same applies in bars 37–40.

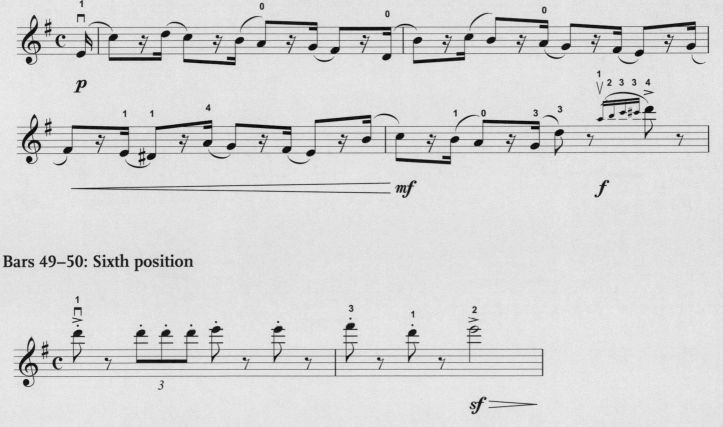

Bars 49–50: Sixth position

March Of The Toys

Music by Pyotr Ilyich Tchaikovsky

Tempo di marcia ♩ = 144

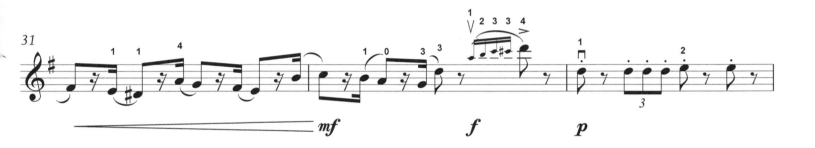

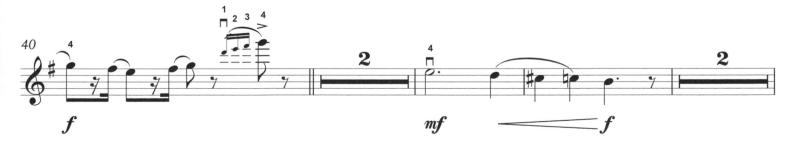

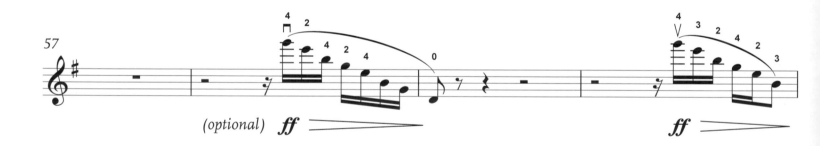

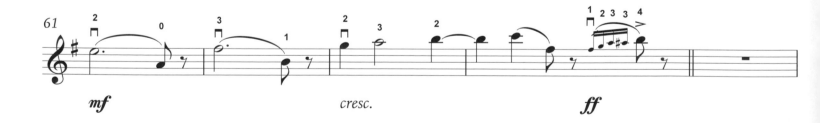

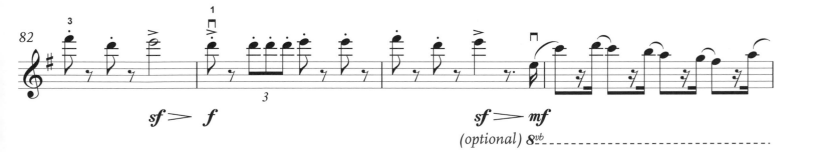

(optional) *8vb* -

Jeeves And Wooster

Anne Dudley's theme for the much-loved BBC series exudes a spirit of elegance and decadence, which was a way of life for some in the 1930s. At the same time it is charged with a suggestion of drama—Bertie would be about to get into some scrape or other—and it demands a warm, fruity sound.

Choose higher positions on lower strings for the first section (bars 5–20) use plenty of vibrato and make juicy, audible shifts. The composer ratchets up the tension by making the second section a semitone higher than the first and as this flat key is slightly awkward for the violin it may require some extra practice.

Scale shapes to practise

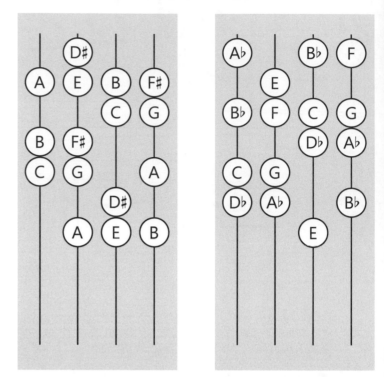

E minor   **F minor**

Practice windows

Bars 6–7, 22, 27, 29–30: Syncopation It is simplest to treat the syncopated notes (always tied in this piece, so they are easy to spot) as coming a swung quaver *early*. You can also practise the rhythms straight, for example, bars 6–7 would be four crotchets followed by a semibreve.

56

Jeeves And Wooster

Music by Anne Dudley

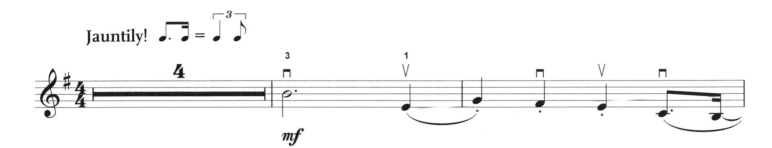

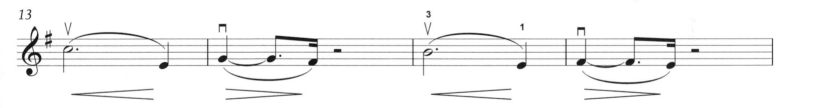

cresc.

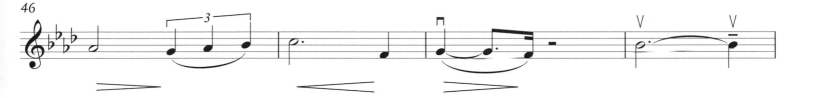

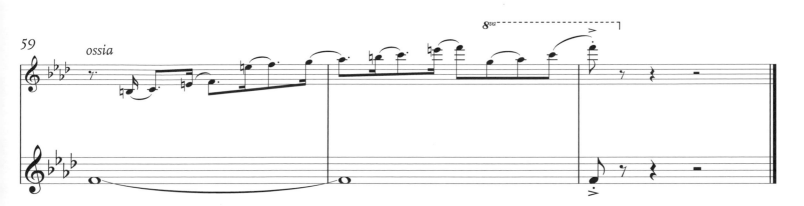

Theory Reminder

Useful terms

A tempo: back to original speed, usually after **rit**. or **rall**.

Accent ($\overset{\cdot}{\smile}$)**:** a sharp attack at the beginning of the note

Adagio: slow, between andante and largo

Al niente: to nothing, to silence, e.g., *dim. al niente*

Allegretto: moderately fast

Allegro: lively

Andante: moderate, walking pace

Bar: unit of music, enclosed by barlines

Beat (or **pulse**)**:** the regular underlying heartbeat of music

Cadenza: a solo section, often used to show off musical technique within a Concerto or similar piece

Cantabile: play in a singing style

Coda ($\oplus$ **Coda**)**:** final section of a piece

Concerto: a piece in three parts consisting of a soloist accompanied by an orchestra

Crescendo or **cresc.** (————————)**:** instruction to get louder

D.S. al Coda: instruction to continue playing from the 𝄋 sign, moving on to the Coda at the $\oplus$ sign

Diatonic: using notes that belong to the current key

Diminuendo or **dim.** (————————)**:** instruction to get softer

Dolce: sweet/gentle

Dynamics: relates to the loudness and softness in music

Espressivo: play expressively

f**:** dynamic marking, loud, stands for *forte*

Glissando: a rapid scale between two notes, often an embellishment

Grace note or **acciaccatura** (♪): a very quick note played before another note

Grave: slow and solemn

Grazioso: gracefully

Intonation: tuning

Largo: very slowly

Lento: slowly

Legato: smooth, connected

Maestoso: play majestically

Meno: less

Metronome: device that provides a steady beat and can be set at different tempos

Minuet: a piece originally from a dance in triple time

Moderato: moderately

Molto: much, a lot

Mosso: with movement

Movement: section of a large composition (e.g. 3rd movement of symphony no. 5)

Multiple-bar rest ($\underline{\quad\overset{4}{\quad}\quad}$): instruction to leave a gap for the amount of bars indicated

Non legato: not smooth

mf: dynamic marking, fairly loud, stands for *mezzo forte*

mp: dynamic marking, fairly soft, stands for *mezzo piano*

Ostinato: a short pattern that is repeated

Overture: a piece used as an introduction to a dramatic, choral or instrumental composition

p: dynamic marking, soft, stands for *piano*

Più: more

Poco: a little

Poco a poco: little by little

Presto: very fast

Rall. (short for **rallentando**): slow down

Rhythm: the patterns of various long and short notes that make up a melody

Rit. (short for **ritardando** or **ritenuto**)**:** slow down

Rondo: a musical form in which one section comes back time and time again

Rubato: a flexible tempo that can be pulled around to suit the style

Slur: curved line over two or more notes, indicating that you should connect the notes and play smoothly

Sonata: instrumental piece for piano, or solo instrument and piano, usually in three movements

Staccato (♩)**:** short and detached

Stringendo: pressing forward or moving on

Subdivision: technique for understanding complex rhythm

Subito, sub. : suddenly

Swing, swung quavers: jazzy rhythm in which quavers are played unevenly, with the first played longer than the second in each group of two

Symphony: a large composition for orchestra often in four movements

Syncopation: rhythm featuring off-beats, often found in jazzy and popular music

Tempo: the speed of a piece of music

Tenuto (♩)**:** play the note's full value, perhaps with a little added emphasis

Time signature: instruction at the start of music giving information on its rhythmic foundation

Treble clef (𝄞)**:** sign at the beginning of all violin music, also used for piano right hand, which indicates that you play in a treble, or high, range

Triplet: three notes of any rhythmic value to be played in the space of two, indicated by a number '3' over the notes

Troppo: too much

Tutti: all, used to indicate where everyone plays together

Vibrato: a technique of the left hand and arm in which the pitch of a note varies in a pulsating rhythm. This is achieved by rocking the hand back and forth while the finger is pressing down the note, which gives the note a fuller and richer sound

Vivace: lively and fast

Accidentals (alter the pitch of notes)

♯ **Sharp:** raises the pitch of any note by a semitone

♭ **Flat:** lowers the pitch of any note by a semitone

♮ **Natural:** cancels out the effect of a sharp or flat

𝄪 **Double Sharp:** raises the pitch of any note by a whole tone

♭♭ **Double Flat:** lowers the pitch of any note by a whole tone

Note values

○ ▬ **Semibreve:** (whole note), or rest of equivalent length, lasts for four beats

♩ ▬ **Minim:** (half note), or rest of equivalent length, lasts for two beats

♩ 𝄽 **Crotchet:** (quarter note), or rest of equivalent length, lasts for a quarter of a semibreve and is commonly used as a one-beat note

♪ 𝄾 **Quaver:** (eighth note), or rest of equivalent length, lasts for half a beat

♬ 𝄿 **Semiquaver:** (sixteenth note), or rest of equivalent length, lasts for a quarter of a beat

♬ 𝅀 **Demisemiquaver:** (thirty-second note), or rest of equivalent length, lasts for an eighth of a beat

♩. 𝄽· **Dot:** increases the length of a note or rest by 50%

⌣ **Tie:** joins two notes together — the duration of the second is added to the first

Time signatures

Simple time		Compound time		Unusual time signatures	
$\frac{2}{4}$	2 crotchet beats in a bar	$\frac{6}{8}$	6 quaver beats in a bar	$\frac{5}{8}$	5 quaver beats in a bar
$\frac{3}{4}$	3 crotchet beats in a bar	$\frac{9}{8}$	9 quaver beats in a bar	$\frac{7}{8}$	7 quaver beats in a bar
$\frac{4}{4}$	4 crotchet beats in a bar	$\frac{12}{8}$	12 quaver beats in a bar	$\frac{11}{8}$	11 quaver beats in a bar
$\frac{3}{2}$	3 minim beats in a bar				

RESTART VIOLIN CD TRACK LISTING

FULL INSTRUMENTAL PERFORMANCES

1. **THE CAN CAN**
(OFFENBACH)
DORSEY BROTHERS MUSIC LIMITED

2. **LARGO**
(DVOŘÁK)
DORSEY BROTHERS MUSIC LIMITED

3. **YESTERDAY**
(LENNON/McCARTNEY)
SONY/ATV MUSIC PUBLISHING (UK) LIMITED

4. **ENTR'ACTE**
(SCHUBERT)
DORSEY BROTHERS MUSIC LIMITED

5. **CABARET**
(EBB/KANDER)
CARLIN MUSIC CORPORATION

6. **POR UNA CABEZA**
(GARDEL/LE PERA)
DORSEY BROTHERS MUSIC LIMITED

7. **CLAIR DE LUNE**
(DEBUSSY)
DORSEY BROTHERS MUSIC LIMITED

8. **A LOVE BEFORE TIME**
(DUN)
SONY/ATV MUSIC PUBLISHING (UK) LIMITED

9. **I GOT RHYTHM**
(GERSHWIN)
DORSEY BROTHERS MUSIC LIMITED

10. **SOMEONE TO WATCH OVER ME**
(GERSHWIN)
DORSEY BROTHERS MUSIC LIMITED

11. **MARCH OF THE TOYS**
(TCHAIKOVSKY)
DORSEY BROTHERS MUSIC LIMITED

12. **JEEVES AND WOOSTER**
(DUDLEY)
BUFFALO MUSIC LIMITED/UNIVERSAL MUSIC PUBLISHING LIMITED

BACKING TRACKS ONLY

13. **THE CAN CAN**
14. **LARGO**
15. **YESTERDAY**
16. **ENTR'ACTE**
17. **CABARET**
18. **POR UNA CABEZA**
19. **CLAIR DE LUNE**
20. **A LOVE BEFORE TIME**
21. **I GOT RHYTHM**
22. **SOMEONE TO WATCH OVER ME**
23. **MARCH OF THE TOYS**
24. **JEEVES AND WOOSTER**